Anger Management
in a week

DR SANDI MANN

Hodder Arnold

A MEMBER OF THE HODDER HEADLINE GROUP

Order queries: please contact Bookpoint Ltd, 39 Milton Park, Abingdon, Oxon
Orders: please contact Bookpoint Ltd, 130 Milton Park, Abingdon, Oxon OX14
4SB. Telephone: (44) 01235 827720. Fax: (44) 01235 400454. Lines are open from
9.00–18.00, Monday to Saturday, with a 24 hour message answering service.
You can also order through our website www.hoddereducation.com

British Library Cataloguing in Publication Data
A catalogue record for this title is available from the British Library

ISBN 0 340 81630 9

First published   2004
Impression number   10 9 8 7 6 5 4 3 2
Year   2008 2007 2006 2005

Copyright © 2004 Sandi Mann

Typeset by SX Composing DTP, Rayleigh, Essex.
Printed in Great Britain for Hodder Education, a division of Hodder
Headline, 338 Euston Road, London NW1 3BH by Cox & Wyman Ltd., Reading.

Hodder Headline's policy is to use papers that are natural, renewable and
recyclable products and made from wood grown in sustainable forests. The
logging and manufacturing processes are expected to conform to the
environmental regulations of the country of origin

C O N T E N T S

We are all becoming angrier. Over the past decade, our expectations have risen in line with the 'compensation culture' that is becoming an endemic part of 21st century life. If things are not perfect, we are learning that we have the right to demand that they be put right. Thus, things that we accepted in the past now make us angry, especially when our demands are not met in the way we have come to expect. This all contributes to a less tolerant, angrier society.

At work this manifests itself in two main ways: we are angrier and so are the people we work with, particularly the customers. It takes less to provoke us and others around us to anger, and that anger in turn is more likely to lead to aggression or rage. The problem with anger at work is that it is not generally considered to be an acceptable emotion to display. This means that if we express it, we risk consequences, perhaps even disciplinary action. If we suppress it, the anger bubbles below the surface causing us stress and, in all likelihood, a displaced eruption of rage at the supermarket checkout ('trolley rage'), in the car ('car rage') or on the phone to the bank ('phone rage').

Anger Management In a Week is not about eliminating anger, but about helping you to become less angry in general so that you need more provocation to become angry. The book should help you to recognise when it is appropriate to feel angry and how to express that anger appropriately. Various anger management techniques are presented so that you can develop your own tool-box of skills to draw on when appropriate. The book also helps you to manage the anger of other people such as colleagues, the boss and, of course, customers, as well as helping you to handle that most extreme (and dangerous) form of rage, aggression.

The nature of workplace anger

Before we can start to address anger management in the
workplace, it is useful to understand what anger is and the
effects it can have (and to differentiate it from related
concepts such as aggression). Today we will concentrate on
discussing the increasing relevance of anger to worklife, and
on recognising when anger at work is a problem for you.
Issues covered include:

- Understanding what anger is
- The most common sources of anger in the
  workplace
- Differentiating anger from aggression, frustration and
  rage
- Understanding the effects anger has on the body
- Recognising the signs that your anger is a problem
  at work

What is anger?

Like most human emotions, anger is usually a healthy part of
our emotional repertoire. When we feel angry, this is our
body's way of signalling that something is wrong, that we
are not happy and that we need to take action. Historically,
our ancestors' anger would have alerted them to the fact that,
for example, a rival was stealing food or prized possessions;
the strong feelings generated by the emotion would have
stimulated the victim to fight for their rights and their
possessions. The emotional response would have created
physiological changes in the body (see p. 12) which would

produce extra strength, resources and energy to fight.
Without that strength of feeling, our cave-dwelling ancestors
would have been too laid-back to be bothered with
aggressors or rivals and would not have survived long.

The causes of our anger may be different now, but the
strength of feeling is still just as powerful in many people. If,
for instance, we are being taken advantage of at work, anger
motivates us to take action. Anger then, can be a very
important emotion, despite the bad press that it receives; it
motivates us to take action against perceived unfairness, it
signals to us that a wrong has been committed, and it draws
our (and others') attention to problems that need to be
addressed. The difficulty is that we can rarely deal with our
anger by the physical means available to our less civilised
ancestors; today, dealing with anger is far more complex and
has to obey the 'rules of engagement' of the society we live in.

This is no more true than at work. Work is probably the
most prescribed arena in terms of which emotions we are

expected to display and which we are expected to suppress. At home with our partners, with our friends, even in the supermarket, we are relatively free to express our feelings, safe in the knowledge that our loved ones will put up with it or that we need never see strangers at the supermarket again. At work, however, our relationships are not usually so intimate that our colleagues will tolerate outbursts – and, of course, we will see our co-workers again and have to live with any consequences of any emotional outburst.

Workplaces are traditionally rational places. Emotional reactions, nuances, hunches, intuition – none of these are generally considered to have a part to play in the rational enterprise that we call work. Certainly, emotions are well controlled in most work environments by *display rules*; these are (usually) unwritten rules that specify which emotions ought to be expressed and which suppressed. Unsurprisingly, extremes of emotional display are discouraged as are negative emotions like fear, disappointment and anger.

Yet research suggests that emotions like anger, which organisations try to suppress, don't go away. According to a report by Donald Gibson of Fairfield University and Sigal Barsade of Yale University,[1] one out of four employees is substantially angry at work, with half claiming to feel at least 'a little angry' at work. This anger, Gibson and Barsade suggest, leads to a sapping of energy and job satisfaction at work. My own research suggests that anger is the most commonly suppressed negative emotion at work, suppressed in around 10 per cent of all workplace interactions. Whilst the causes of workplace anger will be discussed in more detail on Friday, it is useful to outline here some of the more common things that make us angry at work:

[1] Gibson, D.E. and Barsade, S.G. (1999) *The Experience of Anger at Work: Lessons from the Chronically Angry*, presented at the Academy of Management, Chicago, Illinois.

- Others stealing our ideas
- Not being consulted or involved in decisions affecting us
- Practical problems that block our goals such as parking difficulties or the daily commute
- Colleagues letting us down
- Business contacts not returning our calls
- Technological failures such as computer crashes
- Malicious gossip
- Unfair treatment, e.g. the type or quantity of work allocated to us
- Feeling of betrayal by the organisation

In general, all of these sources of anger fall into one of four main themes:

- Frustrations that block us from doing what we want to
- Irritations such as noise or disruptions
- Abuse
- Injustice

Frustration, anger, aggression and rage

Whilst most of us know what anger is, many of us confuse it with aggression and frustration. It is useful to separate these terms to help understand them and their relationship to anger. *Frustration* is often a precursor to anger; it is the feeling we experience when we don't get what we want, when obstacles are put in our way or when someone interferes with our attempts at achieving our goals. At work, telephone interruptions, colleagues popping by for a chat, the computer server being slow and the photocopier breaking down are all the sorts of frustrations that can easily build to create workplace anger.

Aggression, on the other hand, is the action that can result from the feeling of being angry. It is usually intended to cause physical or emotional harm to others, perhaps with verbal insults, threats, sarcasm or raised voices. When aggression becomes so extreme that we lose self-control, it is said that we are in a *rage*. Such a person is characterised by being very loud – shouting or screaming – red in the face, shaking, threatening and perhaps even physically abusive.

Clearly the workplace environment is not the place for rage, which is likely to lead to disciplinary action. Extreme displays of anger are rarely tolerated at work which means that we have either to find appropriate ways of expressing our feelings (many of which will be outlined later in this book, in particular on Tuesday), or we must suppress them altogether. Both expression and suppression of anger at work have potentially negative outcomes for the individual and for those around them. Let us turn then, to the effects that anger has on us.

How does anger affect us?

Anger, like stress and other powerful emotions, has a profound effect on the body. As our anger rises, the hypothalamus in the brain stimulates the pituitary glands to release a range of hormones that affect every part of our body in one way or another. The main players are adrenaline and cortisol, and these exert their influence via the cardiovascular system and other organs. Adrenaline causes the heart to beat faster and blood pressure to rise; this allows oxygenated blood to flow to areas of the body that are responsible to reacting to the source of anger. Traditionally, the areas needing the extra energy would be the limbs (to run or fight) and the brain (to think faster), whilst blood is diverted from other less important areas like the stomach. Extra energy is also provided by the release of extra sugar or glucose into the blood.

The net effect of all this hormonal activity is a rapid heartbeat, breathlessness (as the lungs struggle to take in more oxygen), high blood pressure and a raised body

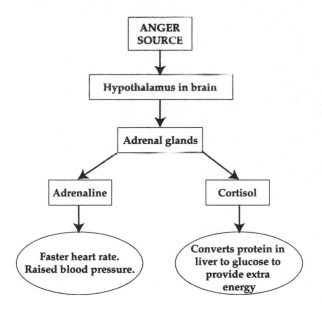

Symptom	Why does it occur?
Aching limbs	The build-up of glucose in the limbs can make our arms and legs feel heavy and tired. In addition, we tend to tense our muscles in preparation for flight or fight and this tension causes pain.
Headache	Blood supply increases to the brain to enable us to think more clearly, but build-up causes headaches.
Neckache	Again, we tend to tense our neck muscles when stressed, causing pain.
Tiredness	We feel tired because we have been burning up so much extra energy.
Dry mouth	Flow of saliva is reduced to the mouth.
Stomach ache/ Butterflies	Blood is diverted away from this area so digestive mechanisms are reduced – this can lead to digestive problems and discomfort.
Dizziness	Although we breathe more quickly when we are feeling angry or emotional, we tend to take more shallow breaths and thus we do not breathe in as much oxygen as we do normally. This can lead to a slightly reduced supply to the brain, causing dizziness.

temperature (due to increasing energy expenditure). All this made our angry ancestors ideally placed to deal with the source of their anger as they used up new reserves of energy to, for example, fight rivals for scarce food resources.

At work, the physiological effects of anger are less useful. Rarely do we have the chance to respond to the source of our anger in the way that our body reactions have designed us to. Rather than turn to aggression, we are much more likely to suppress our emotions either totally or partially as we try to produce a more socially acceptable response. The result of this emotion management is that the anger does not really dissipate and the hormones continue to surge around our body. This results in a range of symptoms affecting our whole body.

Feeling and suppressing anger has specifically been linked to a variety of health complaints including job stress, heart disease, high blood pressure and anxiety. Even expressing anger is thought to be highly stress inducing (despite commonly-held views that it is cathartic to release anger). Expressing anger, of course, affects other people at work and can lead to what Gibson and Barsade call 'breaches in interpersonal relationships and a hostile work environment'.

Recognising the signs that your anger at work is a problem

As indicated earlier, anger is not necessarily a 'bad' emotion that must be eliminated at work. Like all emotions, it serves a purpose and, expressed appropriately, can have positive outcomes at work such as enabling us to stand up for ourselves or motivating us to speak out against injustices. It is only a problem when anger is:

1 Chronic (you are always angry and it doesn't take much to send you into a rage); or
2 Inappropriately expressed (in explosive, aggressive or other unacceptable ways); or
3 Too intense (high intensity of anger rarely produces positive results since we are more likely to say or do things we regret, we think less clearly and we may act impulsively); or
4 Lasting too long.

Use the following exercise to see if anger at work is a problem for you. Read the statements and tick the number that corresponds to the way you feel about each item using the following scale:

1	2	3	4	5
Very infrequently	Infrequently	Sometimes	Frequently	Very frequently

1 I find myself wishing that I could exact some nasty revenge on my boss/colleague/client.

1	2	3	4	5

2 I find myself making negative references to a collective group of people I work with (e.g. 'stupid patients', 'those idiots in accounts', 'pathetic customers').

1	2	3	4	5

3 I feel that I am treated unfairly at work.

1	2	3	4	5

4 I don't feel I get the respect I deserve at work.

1	2	3	4	5

5 It doesn't take much to push me over the edge at work in terms of losing my temper.

1	2	3	4	5

6 Colleagues ask me to stop shouting or to calm down.

1	2	3	4	5

7 I feel that there are many things at work that happen to me that are out of my control.

1	2	3	4	5

8 I feel angry.

1	2	3	4	5

9 I fantasise about people I work with getting their 'just deserts'.

1	2	3	4	5

10 I slam doors or slam the phone down.

1	2	3	4	5

11 I find myself taking my anger out on my partner.

1	2	3	4	5

12 I have grudges against people at work.				
1	2	3	4	5
13 I am frightened about what I might do if I really lose it at work.				
1	2	3	4	5
14 I am considered an 'angry person' at work.				
1	2	3	4	5
15 I feel that expressing anger aggressively (e.g. very loudly) is probably the best way to get through to people.				
1	2	3	4	5
16 I use physical actions (such as slamming my hand on the table, or jabbing my finger towards someone) when I am angry.				
1	2	3	4	5
Total score =				

The higher the score, the more likely it is that you could have a problem with managing your anger at work. Scores over 40 certainly indicate a problem. There are many techniques that you can use to control your anger in terms of expressing it appropriately and dealing with any suppressed anger in a healthy way. We will start to look at various aspects of anger management on Tuesday, but tomorrow we will focus on the 'angry personality' and ways of becoming less angry in general.

Summary

Today we have started to really understand workplace anger, its effects on our bodies and our susceptibility to it. Tomorrow we will examine ways to reduce the risks of getting angry by becoming calmer and less 'threat sensitive' in general.

The 'angry personality' – and what to do about it

Many people ask if there is such a thing as an 'angry personality'. The bad news is that there are people who are more 'threat sensitive' than others; their personality and genetic make-up (as well as learned experiences throughout their lives) make them more likely to get angry without needing much provocation. The good news is that this trait can be changed and angry people can become much calmer in general. Today, we will look at ways to achieve this by focusing on:

- Cognitive factors – how we think
- Affective factors – how we feel
- Behavioural factors – how we act

Yesterday we talked about the main themes that cause us to be angry, which are frustrations, irritations, abuse and injustice. These are external events and on their own do not necessarily make us angry. Thus, the same people can be exposed to the same irritations and frustrations, but some will remain calm, some will become slightly angry and others will be hot with rage. The reason for these different responses is tied into our personality traits, which can make us easier or harder to provoke. These traits are to do with the ways in which we think, feel and behave, and are often learned through exposure to particular events or experiences. These ways of responding to provocation become ingrained but, with some effort, they can be changed.

Cognitive factors

Cognitive factors that contribute to an angry personality refer to our mental processes and include:

1 *Our interpretation of events*: events are only anger-eliciting if we appraise them or interpret them to be so. This is why people can experience the same events but only some of us will interpret them in ways that make us feel angry. We talk of people taking things 'too personally' or in psychological terms, of being too 'threat sensitive'.

2 *Our expectations*: when our expectations are very high, we can end up irritated and frustrated, which can lead to anger. We expect things to be perfect, to go well or for others to reach our high standards and, when they don't, we get angry.

Changing the cognitive aspects that contribute towards an angry personality involves changing the way we interpret our world, and altering the expectations we hold. A good way to start tackling these cognitive factors is to start keeping an 'anger diary'. Take a notebook or A4 notepad and use the following questions as a template for each angry event within your diary.

What happened exactly?	
What thoughts were going through your mind?	
What was your response? (e.g. showed no anger, walked away, became aggressive, etc.)	
How angry did you feel on a scale of 1–10?	
Who or what were you angry with? (e.g. myself, a customer/colleague, an object, etc.)	

Keep the anger diary at work for several weeks and see what pattern starts to emerge. This diary will be referred to throughout this chapter, but for the moment we are particularly interested in the second question: 'What thoughts were going through your mind?' It is this question that will help you to identify your cognitive mind-sets to see if your interpretations and expectations are appropriate. Look at the events that made you angry in your diary, and ask yourself whether these events made (or whether they are likely to make) others just as angry. If not, it could be that you are interpreting things too negatively or too personally. Try to change the way you think and interpret events. Ask yourself how you could have interpreted the event differently, and make a conscious effort to be more objective when you interpret potentially provocative events. Now, go back to your diary and concentrate on changing or *reframing* your interpretation of events.

Much of the change that you will need to effect will involve transforming negative thoughts to more positive ones. This is sometimes called 'cognitive restructuring' and involves restructuring or changing your common cognitions or thoughts. The first step is to catch yourself with these negative cognitions or 'cognitive distortions', and then to replace them with more positive ones. Catch the negative cognitions by checking for:

Event	Old interpretation	New interpretation
Boss rubbished my ideas in a staff meeting.	How dare he treat me like that! He thinks I am stupid and that my ideas are worthless!	That is just his manner – he treats other people in the same way.
The computer keeps crashing and I have a deadline to meet.	This always happens to me. It's typical. Whenever I have something important to do, everything conspires against me.	Actually, if I am objective, it just _seems_ like this always happens to me. It happens to other people too and actually it has not happened to me for ages.
I am so fed up with people not returning my calls, or being "in a meeting" when I call.	Nobody values me – I am not worth calling. It is no wonder that no one returns my calls – I am pathetic.	This is typical of some people and is more about them than me. Other people in my office have exactly the same problem.

- *Exaggeration*: this is when you see things as worse than they really are, or you imagine that terrible things will result from minor events. For example, a customer threatens to complain about you and you immediately imagine that you will be fired. Reframe this by looking for the positive. So, for instance, a rude customer could present a good opportunity to practise your new anger management skills! Another form of exaggeration is to always see anger-eliciting events as having the same strength of disaster. For angry people when things go wrong, it is always a 'nightmare' or 'disastrous' and makes them 'furious'. Such people need to train themselves to scale their anger (using the anger diary template provided earlier (p. 21) is a good start) so that they can differentiate between those events that are only mildly annoying or irritating and those that have more serious implications.
- *Generalisation*: this is when, for example, you find yourself saying. 'This always happens to me'. Alter this by thinking of occasions when things have gone well; it is the negative events that we remember most, so you may need to work at this.
- *Irrationality*: many of our cognitions are not rational in that there is no evidence to support them. Thus, we feel angry that an event has happened to us as if we are the only ones that this happens to; this is probably irrational, and fuels our anger. Refute irrational ideas by asking yourself if there is any rational support or evidence for the interpretation you have made of an event.
- *Filtering*: this involves selecting out and focusing on one negative aspect of a situation and ignoring any positive aspects. This is a common feature of the angry personality. For instance, you may have satisfied customers all

morning but you only focus on the one rude one. Or you may have had a reasonable day but one thing goes wrong and you forget about all that has gone well. To counter this, you need to refocus on all that has gone well and put the frustrating event in perspective.

- *Misattribution*: many angry people are quick to make negative and egocentric attributions about events that less angry people would not. For example, when something happens that thwarts their goals (such as a colleague letting them down) or that seems unfair (such as the boss giving a plum job to a colleague), the angry individual attributes the event to some personal and deliberate slight against them – 'She has let me down deliberately' or, 'My boss doesn't think I am up to the job'. Less angry people might attribute other less negative explanations for these events such as, 'My colleague made a mistake', or, 'My boss has given the plum job to someone else this time but that could be because I was not available when she was allocating the work', and thus they feel less angry.

In terms of expectations, how do you know if you simply hold high standards or if the expectations you set are unrealistic? The acid test is really whether you are continually disappointed and irritated by others failing to meet your expectations. Having high standards is admirable, but not if holding them is unhealthy for you. If lowering your general expectations in life will help manage your anger then this might be a trade-off worth accepting.

Affective factors

Affective factors that can contribute towards an angry personality include:

1 *Levels of tension*: people who are generally more tense, anxious or stressed are more easily provoked. When we are tense, it does not take much to send us over the edge. Minor set-backs are seen as catastrophes and small irritations become major grievances.

2 *Taking things too seriously*: linked in with tension is the issue of becoming too serious about things, and being unable to distance ourselves enough to put things in perspective. We may find that we don't laugh as much as we used to or we seem to have lost our sense of humour. Things that we might have laughed at or shrugged off before now make us angry instead.

The key to reducing the affective factors that contribute towards an angry personality is to relax. You can't be angry and relaxed at the same time – the two states are incompatible (we will cover this more fully on Wednesday). Reducing your general levels of stress and tension by becoming more relaxed will lead to you needing more provocation to lose your temper. You will not get so angry over small things. You will be better able to control your responses to conflict and confrontation.

Look again at your anger diary, and particularly at the situations that have been causing you anger. Are they major events that would challenge the patience of a saint? Or are many of the anger-eliciting events things that wouldn't normally get you so wound up?

Learning how to relax is a major life skill and there are numerous ways to approach it. Deep Muscle Relaxation Therapy (sometimes called progressive muscle relaxation therapy) can be very effective because it teaches you to relax each muscle in your body and to recognise when tension is starting to build (see Thursday's chapter) The tension in our bodies reflects the tension in our minds and learning to reduce this physical tension can be very effective. There are many books and tapes available to help learn these techniques.

Other relaxation techniques include sport and exercise, yoga and meditation – anything that helps you to become a calmer, more relaxed person.

You should also be examining your lifestyle to see if there are other ways in which you could become more relaxed. A major element of a stressful lifestyle is poor time management; a common symptom of which is ever-increasing frustration and irritation. If your angry personality is largely caused by ineffective time management skills, you may have other symptoms:

- Constantly rushing
- Often being late for meetings, etc.
- Often feeling impatient
- Chronically vacillating between alternative courses of action
- Procrastination
- Forgetfulness, e.g. neglecting to bring required documents to meetings

All of this can contribute to your general stress levels as well as building up your levels of frustration and irritation until it takes very little to send you into a rage. Again, there are many books on time management, most of which help you to clarify your values, set priorities, set goals, combat procrastination, develop action plans and evaluate how you spend your time.

Behavioural factors

People tend to develop stereotyped ways of responding to events – sometimes called 'scripts'. This is why we often know how others will react to bad news – because we know their typical response pattern. There are two general styles of behaviour that can contribute towards the angry personality:

1 *Avoidance response*: This is when the individual does not deal with the conflict but withdraws and walks away. This might seem like a good option because it appears to be a peaceful response, but it is passive and results in several negative consequences:

  - The conflict remains unresolved

- Because the provocation remains, the anger does not have a chance to dissipate
- Being passive can affect our self-worth and we feel like we are being treated like a doormat, being walked all over or being down-trodden.
- Anger that is not directed outwards can easily become directed inwards, towards ourselves. If this occurs frequently or continually, it can eventually lead to depression.

2 *Hostility response*: this is when the individual reacts with hostility or aggression to the provocation. This response is generally counter-productive in that the victim of the outburst often increases their own anger, leading to an increasing anger cycle. Aggression is poorly tolerated at work, so this response is incompatible with a successful work life.

The key to effective anger management responses is in being assertive. The two response patterns described above are

passive and aggressive responses, whereas the effective
response is to deal assertively with the problem in a way that
acknowledges the rights of those that provoke you and your
own rights. We will be dealing with this tomorrow.

Summary

Today we have examined the factors that contribute towards
the angry personality and looked at ways of becoming less
angry in general. If we can reduce our proneness to anger, we
reduce our chances of letting anger overcome us; we become
more resistant to provocation. Tomorrow we will begin to
explore more specific anger management tools which will
help you to learn to express your workplace anger
appropriately.

Expressing workplace anger appropriately

Yesterday we looked at ways of reducing anger levels in order to become less angry in general. This should help increase resistance to provocation, and today we begin the first of the chapters examining different techniques of anger management. We will focus on using assertion training to learn to express workplace anger appropriately and will cover:

- The right to be angry
- Assertive anger scripts
- Assertive anger language

The right to be angry

This book is not about eliminating anger. It is entitled 'Anger Management' and it is important to understand and accept that this does not mean that the aim is to stop you either being angry or showing your anger. As discussed on Sunday, anger can serve a valuable purpose and should not be seen as totally negative. By anger *management* we mean ensuring anger is:

- Less disruptive
- Less aggressive
- Less likely to impact on our work life
- Less likely to impact on our health

The aim should be to learn to feel and express anger appropriately at work rather than to suppress it or express it in a way that is detrimental either to ourselves or those we work with.

The first stage to successful anger management is to become aware of your rights with regards to anger. Many people are aware of the idea of having rights in terms of being assertive. These rights include such statements as:

- The right to have an opinion
- The right to say 'No'
- The right to ask for what I want
- The right to make mistakes
- The right to put myself first sometimes
- The right to change my mind
- The right to protest against unfair treatment or criticism

For many people with anger problems at work, the difficulties lie in either suppressing or expressing the anger too much, with too much intensity or frequency. Many of these issues are linked to assertiveness – people who are not assertive enough can either be too passive (leading to too much suppression) or too aggressive (leading to too much expression). People who are too passive are often not aware enough of their own rights whilst those who are too aggressive lack awareness of the rights of other people.

You are being assertive when you stand up for these rights, but in such a way as to recognise the rights of others. Consequently, part of being assertive is to accept that others

have the same rights. People generally use one of three
interpersonal styles with regards to asserting their rights:

- *Passive style*: this is when people fail to express their rights
  adequately, perhaps because they cannot really accept that
  they have the same rights as other people (often due to low
  self-esteem). Passive people find it hard to say 'No' and
  they do things they do not want to because they feel that
  others are more important than themselves, and have a
  greater right to assert themselves. They find it hard to put
  themselves first, hard to stand up for themselves when
  criticised, and feel that they must always please others.
  Such people may feel frustrated at being so passive, and
  this style can adversely affect their self-esteem. Passive
  people find it very hard to express their anger and are
  constantly preoccupied with wondering whether they are
  entitled to be angry in a given situation and, if so, how to
  express that anger without causing offence. At work, this
  means that they are likely to be given the unpopular jobs,

to take too much on, and to find it hard to stand up to their boss or co-workers.

- *Aggressive style*: here, people are well aware of their own rights, but often express them in a way that violates the rights of others. This can be quite a confrontational style that rides roughshod over people's feelings. Aggressive people come across as arrogant and superior, and can seem frightening or threatening (especially to more passive colleagues). They are less worried about pleasing other people or about the impression they create and more concerned with making sure that they are not being treated as doormats. Aggressive people are usually very good at expressing their anger but do so in a manner that wins enemies not friends. The aggressive style is rarely acceptable at work (although that depends on the organisational culture because some are more tolerant of this style than others), and aggression which appears or is threatening is likely to attract disciplinary consequences.

- *Assertive style*: people who express their rights assertively do so in a way that ensures that they accept their own rights as well as those of other people. They accept that they cannot please everyone all the time and that sometimes they will have to put their own needs first. At the same time, they realise that other people have an equal right to want to put their own needs first and to say 'No' to any requests if they wish. Assertive people are able to express their anger when it is appropriate to do so, but in a way that is not threatening to others.

Before exploring the techniques of anger management, it is useful to get a picture of your ability to appropriately express your anger at work. The following self-assessment quiz will help you to identify your anger style in terms of being passive or aggressive. Use the scale to indicate your strength of agreement or disagreement with each statement.

1	2	3	4	5
Strongly disagree	Disagree	Neither agree nor disagree	Agree	Strongly agree

1 I am often unsure as to whether I am entitled to be angry or not.				
1	2	3	4	5
2 I often suppress my anger at work.				
1	2	3	4	5
3 I always seem to be letting off steam at work.				
1	2	3	4	5
4 I am not afraid to show my anger at work.				
1	2	3	4	5
5 There are some people at work who really intimidate me.				
1	2	3	4	5

6 I am afraid to show my anger at work.				
1	2	3	4	5
7 People at work would be disappointed in me if I became angry.				
1	2	3	4	5
8 I point at people a lot when I am angry.				
1	2	3	4	5
9 People often tell me to, 'Calm down' at work.				
1	2	3	4	5
10 People often seem to be backing away from me when I am angry.				
1	2	3	4	5
11 It is really important to me that everyone at work likes me.				
1	2	3	4	5

Passive score: Total score for statements 1, 2, 5, 6, 7 and 11 ☐
Scores over 24 indicate this as your dominant style.

Aggressive score: Total score for statements 3, 4, 8, 9, 10 ☐
Scores over 20 indicate this as your dominant style.

In order to be assertive with our expression of anger we need to recognise our rights in relation to anger at work. This is particularly important for passive people who frequently find it hard to understand whether they have a right to be angry or not in a given workplace situation. Our anger rights at work include:

Anger rights	Examples
The right to feel angry if I have been unfairly treated	• A colleague criticises you without justification • The boss gives preferential jobs to others

The right to feel angry if my needs (which I have expressed assertively) are ignored	• Colleagues are noisy in the office even when you have asked them to be quieter • You have repeatedly requested information from colleagues that is not forthcoming
The right to feel angry if co-workers let me down	• A colleague fails to pass on a phone message • A colleague does not pull their weight in the team
The right to feel angry if a customer is rude to me	• A customer hurls personal insults at you • A customer swears at you or raises their voice
The right to feel angry if anyone at work is aggressive towards me	• A colleague shouts at you and makes you feel intimidated • Your boss swears at you or makes you feel threatened
The right to express my anger assertively at work	• By telling your co-worker that you are angry • By explaining how a customer's actions make you feel

Once you accept that you have these rights with regards to workplace anger, you will realise that your anger 'management' is not about suppressing it or trying to stop yourself feeling angry; on the contrary, appropriate anger management is about *recognising when your rights have been violated, allowing you to acknowledge your anger and expressing that anger assertively when it is appropriate to do so.* Expressing anger assertively is a learned skill that involves the use of both assertive anger scripts and assertive anger language.

Assertive anger scripts

If something or someone has made you angry at work, the first step is to acknowledge your feelings. Once you recognise that you are angry (and not upset or experiencing some other emotion that is easy to confuse with anger), you should check your anger rights (see pp. 36–37). Only then should you think about expressing this anger. Ideally, you will make an appointment or arrange a meeting with the person you are angry with. Of course, there will be occasions when you will not be able to do this and you will have to express your anger there and then. Here is an ideal script or template for assertive anger expression at work:

THAT'S A LOVELY TIE, BUT...

Assertive anger script element	Examples
Begin (and end) on a positive note.	'I really enjoy working with you, but lately . . .' 'I have always found you to be a fair and reasonable manager, but . . .'
Define the problem specifically and early; don't beat about the bush by taking ages to get to the point.	'I want to discuss something with you. I feel that when I make suggestions in meetings, you are not taking them as seriously as I feel you should.'
Use the first person (I) to avoid statements of blame.	'I feel angry' rather than, 'You make me angry'. 'I feel hurt' rather than, 'You have upset me'.
Explain how you feel.	'I feel worried about my job security when I am not kept informed about organisational changes.' 'I am concerned that you will think this is a petty matter, but . . .'
Don't put yourself down.	'I'm probably being too sensitive . . .' 'Perhaps it is just me . . .'
Focus on the main issue and don't get side-tracked by past grievances.	'While we're on the subject . . .' 'Something similar happened six months ago too . . .'
Do criticise the behaviour and not the person.	'I felt aggrieved that you were so noisy when I was trying to make an important call' rather than, 'You are so noisy!'
Avoid generalising.	'You never listen to me!'

Ask for what you want rather than just complain.	'I would like you to keep me informed in future of any developments.' 'I would like you to allow me time to speak in future meetings.'
Make requests realistic. For example, don't ask for too many changes at once or too great a change at once.	'I want you to instigate a policy change about this matter for the whole company by next week.'
Try to demonstrate the positive consequences of your request.	'This will allow me to be a more productive member of the team.' 'This will ensure that none of us miss important calls again.'
Avoid empty threats.	'If you don't do this, I shall be forced to look for employment elsewhere.'

Assertive anger language

Whilst working through your assertive anger scripts, you will need to ensure that your language is neither aggressive nor passive. This includes both your verbal and your non-verbal language. A great deal of communication takes place at the non-verbal level, and this often happens subliminally or subconsciously. We may often be unaware of our own body language and the messages that we are sending out; it is especially important to ensure that if you adopt the assertive anger scripts as detailed above, they are not presented with conflicting body language. If your verbal language says one thing (i.e. assertion) and your body language another (e.g. aggression), it is likely that the overall message will be that of aggression since the non-verbal level of communication is usually more powerful.

Some general points to be aware of in terms of assertive body language include:

- Direct face-to-face stances are seen as more aggressive; try to maintain a slight angle without actually turning away from the other person
- People feel threatened if their personal space is invaded so keep your distance
- Try to keep your hands still; some hand movements (e.g. fist clenching) can be viewed as signs of aggression whilst others (e.g. putting one arm across the chest to clutch at the other arm) are seen as passive

Other specific aspects of anger language, both verbal and non-verbal, are shown in the following table:

	Verbal language	Body language
Aggressive	• Speaks too loudly/shouts • Uses insults or personalises the issues • May swear • Constantly interrupts • Lays blame easily • Uses degrading language	• Waves fists • Points with finger • Has hands on hips • Bangs fists on table • Jabs at other person with finger • Glares • Leans head forward • Leans upper body forward • May invade personal space (gets too close to the other person)
Passive	• Speaks too quietly • Adopts an apologetic tone • Hesitant voice	• Avoids eye contact • Adopts a stooped posture • Bows head • Has 'closed' posture, e.g. with arms folded across chest and/or legs crossed
Assertive	• Speaks clearly • Speaks audibly • May repeat requests	• Maintains direct eye contact • Maintains an upright posture • Has 'open' posture, e.g. with arms by side and legs uncrossed • Keeps distance in order to respect personal space

Summary

Today we have looked at ways of expressing your anger at work appropriately. The first step is recognising when it is legitimate for you to be angry, and this involves an acknowledgement of your anger rights. Then, using assertive anger scripts and language, you can confront the source of your anger and explain what the problem is and how you think it can be resolved. Tomorrow we shall look at the basic tools of anger management.

The basic tools of anger management: cognitive and behavioural approaches

Cognitive and behavioural approaches to anger management involve both the mental processes (our thoughts) and behavioural processes (what we do). We considered some of these approaches on Monday in relation to the angry personality, but today we will look at some specific cognitive and behavioural techniques aimed at controlling our anger at work. These include:

- Avoidance of the provocation
- Distancing yourself from provocation
- Self-disruption of the anger response
- Physical exercise

Avoiding provocation

On Monday, we explored the avoidance response with reference to a negative strategy that contributes to the angry personality (pp. 28–29). It is important to distinguish between avoidance as a maladaptive (i.e. negative) anger management strategy and avoidance as an adaptive (or positive) strategy. The maladaptive avoidance discussed on Monday is when the individual avoids dealing with anger, whereas the strategy to be discussed today is when the individual avoids (or minimises their exposure to) the provocation or the anger-eliciting event. Avoiding dealing with anger can be negative and contribute to the angry personality, as explained on Monday. However, avoiding the anger-eliciting event can be a positive and helpful strategy.

There may be some situations at work that you expect to be provocative and anger-arousing. For example, perhaps there is a particular colleague who always winds you up, a discussion of a sensitive topic that always makes you angry, or a particular type of customer or client group that you know to be difficult. On Monday we discussed starting an anger diary in which you record any anger events. This simply means writing down which events make you angry and in what circumstances, over the period of a few weeks. After several weeks, you may start to see a pattern emerging with certain triggers that are common to much of your anger.

Avoidance as a strategy is clearly not going to be possible for every anger-eliciting event. If dealing with difficult customers is part of your work role, then avoiding this is not possible without changing jobs (which, although a last resort, is an avoidance strategy that should not necessarily be discounted if anger is a major problem for you because of your job role). However, there are some triggers that can be avoided. Read the following case studies about avoidance strategies used by individuals.

Through her anger diaries, Carol found that not being able to find a parking space at her place of work would get her into an angry mood for the whole day. She avoided the parking problem trigger by coming to work an hour earlier and leaving an hour earlier. This necessitated a lifestyle change involving flexitime at work (which she requested and got), going to bed earlier and getting up earlier – both impacting on her home and family life. However, she felt that her new calmness at work made all the changes worthwhile.

For Andy, a common theme to his anger experiences was interruptions. He shared an office with two others and found that the constant interruptions from both his office colleagues and other co-workers were a source of major irritation for him. Typical interruptions involved requests for advice, requests for information and general chatter. He avoided this source of anger by adopting a new 'Please do not disturb' procedure that he explained to all his colleagues; when he placed a red flag on his desk, this meant that he did not wish to be disturbed. He did this for work that needed interruption-free concentration and found that his anger levels dropped considerably.

Sue was a hospital receptionist used to dealing with a wide range of patients, some of whom could be difficult. Some patients would become abusive when they were kept waiting a long time for appointments but, when Sue studied her anger diaries, she discovered that these abusive patients weren't the main trigger for her anger. What really irritated her was the constant stream of patients who seemed to use her as a general information point, needing complicated directions to other departments. Many of these patients struggled to understand her for various reasons (such as language difficulties or difficulties with their hearing), and Sue found it all a drain on her patience. Her avoidance strategy was simply to have a large sign designed and placed in a prominent place directing lost and bewildered patients to a more appropriate reception to be dealt with.

Distancing yourself from the provocation

It is not always possible to avoid the anger triggers, but you may be able to distance yourself from such triggers either physically or temporally. Physical distancing techniques include walking away or moving further away (for example, from an abusive customer), going for a walk to cool down or taking some other physical 'time out'. Temporally distancing yourself is just about using time rather than space as a barrier between the anger-eliciting event and yourself. For instance, you might ask for time to think over an issue to avoid saying something in anger that you might later regret. This is a useful technique if you are not sure of your rights in the situation or you want time to prepare an assertive response (by referring to Tuesday's chapter perhaps!).

Other examples of these techniques in action might be:

- Asking to be excused from an anger-eliciting meeting whilst you calm down and gather your thoughts
- Putting a phone caller on hold whilst you calm down or discuss an appropriate response with a colleague
- Refusing to be drawn into a discussion when you know you are angry, but requesting a later meeting
- Asking for a less confrontational way of discussing a problem, such as using e-mail rather than face to face

Self-disruption of the anger response

There may be instances at work when something makes us really angry, but we feel powerless to do anything about it. We cannot just walk away from the trigger, nor is it something that can be dealt with later. We cannot avoid the situation yet our anger is interfering with our ability to handle it in a calm and rational manner. If it is not possible to avoid the trigger and we cannot moderate it in any way, the only course of action left is within ourselves. We cannot change the event, but we can change the way we react to it. One way to do this is by changing the way we interpret anger-eliciting events, as discussed on Monday. Another way to reduce the significance of the event for us is by interfering with the anger response.

When something makes us angry, our mental processes engage the anger response. This will begin with an appraisal process that will evaluate the trigger to establish whether it is something that has violated our expectations, blocked our attempts at doing something, or in any other way is something that we feel should not have occurred. Moreover, the appraisal process will involve an estimate of the other person's intent to cause harm or distress, and of the degree to which what has happened is justified (fair) or not. Our individual propensity to anger will play a factor in this appraisal, and someone with a low tolerance for frustration will be more likely to feel that they should not have to put up with the event.

The appraisal system will then engage the appropriate level of the anger response which will then kick in. The anger response consists of physiological, emotional and cognitive changes, as explained on Monday. Physiological changes include the release of adrenal hormones; emotional changes include feelings of annoyance, fury and rage; whilst cognitive changes often involve the sort of cognitive biases discussed on Monday (p. 20).

The aim of disrupting the anger response is to break the anger response chain. Self-disruption can occur at various points along the chain: either by reappraising the event (see p. 23) or by preventing the anger response from kicking in.

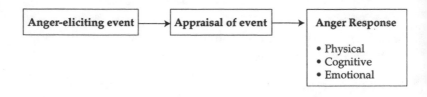

There are several ways to disrupt the anger response:

Engage in incompatible behaviour
Anger is a state of arousal and it is impossible to experience this if you are relaxed. Therefore, if you are able to engage in an activity that makes you feel relaxed, it will be difficult for you to feel anger at the same intensity. One way to achieve a general state of increased relaxation is by learning the skill of Deep Muscle Relaxation Therapy which was mentioned on Monday and will be explained further tomorrow. This is a skill that teaches you how to physically relax your muscles, which can lead to a more relaxed state of mind. By performing relaxation exercises, even short forms of them, you are engaging in behaviour that is incompatible with the anger response. Tomorrow some more specific relaxation

techniques are explored which can be used in response to an angry stimulus or event.

Other things you could try include swimming or sporting activities that you find relaxing, creative or artistic pursuits, looking after pets, or any pastime that you generally find relaxing. Of course, not all of these activities will be accessible to you during the working day, so this technique might be more useful to reduce or limit the anger response at the end of the day (see also Thursday for the use of humour).

Do something distracting
This is a technique aimed at distracting yourself from the anger stimulus and thus reducing the intensity of the anger response. When an event causes us to be angry, we find that we generally never feel as angry as we do the first time that the event happened. Our anger fades, not just with time, but with repeated exposure to the stimulus. This is because our bodies are not capable of maintaining the same level of intense arousal for a long time. This is the case with any

intense arousal, which is why the second ride on a roller-coaster is never as scary as the first, or why an exciting event is never as exciting when repeated. Consequently, if we can distract ourselves from thinking about the anger stimulus, when we think about it again it should not have quite the same hold on us.

Distraction techniques include both physical and mental strategies. Physical distractions include doing some physical activity that occupies your mind (it does not have to be a relaxing activity like in the above technique). So, you could turn your attention to a particular piece of work which requires your concentration, read an interesting newspaper article, or go and talk to somebody about something completely different.

Alexis was fuming about a disparaging comment that a colleague had told her John had made about her. She was so angry that she felt she couldn't think straight. She wanted to have it out with John, but he was in a meeting. After pacing the floor in her office for a while, she decided to distract herself by completing her expense forms. This was a task that she always put off doing because it was time consuming and required concentration – even though it resulted in money for her. She forced herself to work through her expenses and concentrated hard to stop her thinking about John. Knowing that if she didn't concentrate she might make a mistake and not get her money helped to focus her! When she had finished, she found that her anger towards John was more manageable and she was able to confront him in a more assertive way.

Mental distraction techniques include things such as mentally planning a menu for a dinner party, or working out a route to a meeting in another part of town. You may not be physically engaged in a distracting activity, but provided that your mind is distracted this technique can work. An advantage of mental distraction is that it is something that can be done 'here and now' without any need to leave the office or workstation.

Use thought-stopping
This is another cognitive or mental technique that involves you catching the anger response processes and interrupting them. When you feel your anger rising, you interrupt the

anger response by telling yourself to 'Stop' the thoughts from going around your head. When we are angry, we tend to go over and over what has happened in our heads, which causes the anger cues to be continually reinforced.

Thought-stopping as a technique is particularly effective in those situations when there is little we can actually do about the anger event; in other words, nothing productive can come about by continually going over and over something in your mind. Since the anger response is not benefiting anyone, it needs to be stopped, and you can learn to do this by adopting a 'stop' word or sign that is meaningful for you. This might be saying a word like 'Stop', 'Enough' or 'No' to yourself. It could be visualising a stop sign similar to those used for cars on the roads. It could even be a physical sign such as pinching your hand or snapping a rubber band on to your hand. Such signs can be enough to stop the stimulus and to interrupt the anger response.

Physical exercise

Many people report that physical exercise is a useful anger management technique. There are a number of possible reasons for this. One is the misattribution of arousal. When we experience any state of arousal such as anxiety, anger or fear, it is argued that the same feeling underlies any arousal state and it is only our interpretation of that feeling which allows us to label the arousal as 'anger' or 'fear' and so on. If we are exercising, we also experience arousal which we label as that caused by strenuous activity. If we exercise when we are angry, we might lose the 'anger' label and replace it with a physical arousal label.

Another explanation is that strenuous exercise tires us out, and this removes the arousal. It is hard to be very tired and yet also extremely angry, which is why we may hear people comment that, 'I am too tired to care'. A third possibility is that exercise performs a distraction role since our minds are focused on the physical task in hand and complex thought is hindered.

Summary

Today we have started to look at some basic techniques of anger management – skills that you can learn in order to reduce the anger response you are experiencing. Tomorrow we will continue with this theme by looking at some more advanced techniques which require a little more practice to master.

The more advanced tools of anger management

Yesterday we considered some basic techniques that can be used to help you manage or control your own anger in the workplace. Today, we will look at some more advanced techniques that require a little extra skill or practice, but that can become valuable additions to your anger management tool-box.

- Use of self-talk statements
- Relaxation training
- Use of humour
- Channelling anger

Self-talk statements

Sometimes, anger-eliciting events happen which cannot be avoided or for which the strategies outlined yesterday are not appropriate or effective. The use of self-talk statements is a cognitive strategy aimed at either increasing tolerance of the anger-eliciting event, reducing the effect that the event has, or in mobilising other coping strategies. Examples of commonly used self-talk statements include:

Increasing tolerance of the anger-eliciting event

- Worse things can happen
- My anger will pass
- People say things they do not mean when they are angry
- I have to expect these kinds of things to happen

Reducing the effect that the event has

- If I put this event into context of my life, it is not worth getting upset about
- Will I remember this event in five years, or even in one year?
- My health is more important than this so I am not going to let it get to me
- I am not going to give this person the satisfaction of upsetting me – they are not worth it

- In the grand scheme of things, this is not worth getting upset about

Mobilising other coping strategies

- I do not have to let this bother me – I can choose how to react
- There is no point in reacting whilst I am angry – people are not rational in this state and I might say or do something I will regret
- Letting this go is not a sign of weakness

It is useful to study the list above, add your own personal ones (for example, 'I have just had an operation – this event is not important compared to that') and pick out those that you find most helpful. Then, *internalise* the statements by making them part of your everyday cognitive processes. Practise saying them and believing them before an anger-eliciting event happens. You could use visual imagery too, if appropriate, such as imagining your blood bubbling away as your blood pressure rises. By internalising the statements, they will be ready to draw upon when you need them.

Relaxation training

Relaxation has been talked about elsewhere in this book, particularly yesterday when it was mentioned in terms of being a state incompatible with anger. Now, we are going to introduce some specific techniques aimed at inducing a relaxed state which is incompatible with the anger response.

On Monday, the principles of Deep Muscle Relaxation Therapy were outlined; if practised regularly this can help you to become more relaxed in general. This form of relaxation can help to keep general arousal levels lower, so it should take more provocation to get you angry. This technique is aimed at reducing general levels of tension rather than episodic states of tension that occur in response to a specific event or episode. It can be adapted, and a shortened version used in response to anger-eliciting events (see below). However, there are also other relaxation techniques that you can train yourself in so that you will be able to:

- Reduce your levels of anger and arousal in response to an anger-eliciting event
- Be less likely to get aroused in the first place

All relaxation techniques make use of the incompatibility of anger arousal with the state of relaxation.

Progressive relaxation – quick version
Deep Muscle Relaxation Therapy is a form of progressive
relaxation in which you progressively relax your muscles
until you are totally relaxed. This technique can be adapted
to use as a responsive technique when you experience an
anger-eliciting event. If something or someone makes you
really angry, you are obviously not always, or even often,
going to be able to disappear to a quiet place with an easy
chair to engage in a full Deep Muscle Relaxation Therapy
programme. Yet there are quick and unobtrusive ways to
carry out a brief version and this works well if you are
already regularly practising the full version at home.

The key is to tense and relax the main muscle groups rather
than every part of your body. Start off by tensing and
relaxing your arms (including fists, biceps and forearms).
Next move to your back and stomach (tensing and relaxing
once or twice), before finishing with your legs (including toes
and calves). It is also useful to use a trigger word such as
'relax' here and for the full relaxation exercise (see Monday).
If you have already been practising the full technique using
such a trigger word, then saying to yourself the word 'relax'
should act as a kind of Pavlovian trigger to relaxation
because you will have subconsciously learned to associate
that word with the state of relaxation.

Desensitisation
This is a useful technique for situations when you wish to
interrupt the anger response by stopping the anger rather
than avoiding or dealing with the stimulus. In other words,
something has happened that has made you really angry and
there is either nothing you can do about it or you just wish
that you didn't feel so angry about it. Anger is debilitating

and can stop you concentrating on other things. If only you could somehow get that anger to dissipate.

Desensitisation works on the principle that the more you are exposed to a stimulus, the less arousing it will be. This applies to many situations, for instance, phobias are often treated with a graded desensitisation approach that allows the sufferer to gradually come into more and more contact with the feared stimulus until it stops being arousing. Our bodies are designed to *habituate* or become accustomed to arousing stimuli – if we let them. What often happens, specifically with phobias, is that as soon as we get aroused we avoid the stimulus, which does not allow us to build up the resistance.

Therefore, if you cannot get an angry episode out of your mind, and you find it keeps interrupting your work, try a desensitisation approach. If you couple this with relaxation it will be twice as effective. You will, ideally, need a quiet place to do this – it is probably the sort of technique best practised at the end of an 'angry' day:

Lie back in an easy chair and close your eyes. Concentrate on your breathing, which should be slow and steady. Every time you breathe out, say to yourself, 'Relax'. Concentrate on your muscles, and make sure that they are relaxed by tensing and relaxing them each in turn. Now, relive the events that made you so angry. Go through in your mind exactly what happened and how you felt. As you do so, keep your breathing nice and slow and keep saying to yourself, 'Relax' every time you breathe out. As you relive the anger-eliciting event, notice how it makes you feel. Keep reliving the event until it no longer makes you feel so angry. This might take some time, but will eventually happen.

Use of humour

Humour is a cognitive or mental technique that relies on the introduction of something incompatible with the anger response. We talked earlier of behaviours such as relaxation techniques which are incompatible with anger arousal; now we turn our attention to using *affect* or feelings as the incompatible stimulus. The basic premise of using humour is that we cannot feel both angry and amused at the same time. Laughter will thus replace rage. Humour can also be used to put events into perspective by interrupting the appraisal part of the anger response; when we can laugh at something, we interpret the event differently. This is why people may say to

you, 'You'll laugh about this one day' (often when you cannot imagine that day ever coming!). Laughing can also interrupt the anger response by providing an emotional release from the tension.

Using humour in anger-eliciting situations is a skill in itself. The humour should not be hostile, sarcastic or directed at someone with malicious intent. Instead, it is about training yourself to find something funny in what has happened or in what has been said. Examples of humour that can be found within 'angry' situations include:

- The appearance of the other person in an angry encounter; perhaps their face is red with rage, or they look like they are going to 'explode'
- Possibly, in your anger, your words come out wrongly or you get something mixed up (or the other person does)
- Your 'opponent' might use ludicrous insults or exaggerated put-downs

You would probably be wise to refrain from laughing whilst the other person is present as this can really inflame an already fraught situation. However, once the encounter is over, you can relate the story to colleagues or a partner in a way that emphasises the humourous aspect. For example, a colleague was once called a 'cow' even though he is male and he managed to find this amusing rather than insulting.

Channelling anger

In trying to manage, control and reduce our own anger, it is easy to lose sight of the benefits of anger. As mentioned on Sunday, anger is a valuable motivating emotion and, when channelled appropriately, can have great benefits. Parents who have lost children to disease, murder victim relatives and victims of injustice have sometimes channelled their anger into campaigns aimed at improving conditions for others or preventing such things happening again. Anger, when channelled properly, can be the driving force behind positive change for you or others.

Mere acceptance that anger can be a positive force can be enough to reduce the arousal of the situation. In other words, much of the arousal of an angry event is tied to the knowledge that you shouldn't be angry, that anger is bad and that you must try to control it. By turning this on its head and acknowledging not just your right to be angry, but also the benefits that could accrue, much of the internal tension is released, and so taking this cognitive view can in itself offer therapeutic benefits.

Once you have decided to channel your anger, there are two

potential difficulties. The first is knowing what to do with the anger, and the second is staying motivated. We have talked about the fact that states of arousal cannot be continuously perpetuated, and maintaining arousal long enough to take action can sometimes be problematic.

How to channel the anger

When we are very angry it is hard to be rational and objective, yet if we are to channel the anger, rationality is essential. Channelling the anger is about turning what has happened into some kind of positive outcome; either for you as a wronged individual, or for the 'greater good' of humankind (or at least those people in your organisation). Channelling the anger utilises a problem-solving approach.

A good first step is to write down what has happened – something you may already have done if you are keeping an anger diary (see Monday). Then, instead of simply considering the event and its associated emotions and cognitions, consider what could be done to either prevent the event happening in the first place, or to change the outcome of the event. It might be that a different system of organisational or more efficient process could make a difference, or that you could employ a different personal system to prevent a recurrence.

Alice's work involved some overseas travel. Because she worked for a large institution (a university), there was a lot of paperwork to complete, and bureaucracy to wade through in order to get payment and expenses authorised. The university had a system of paying for hotel accommodation direct, so that the employee did not have to pay out large sums and claim them back. This involved giving the details to the finance department to book the accommodation. On one occasion, Alice was about to set off for a conference to St Louis, USA, when she became concerned that she had no confirmation of her hotel booking. It transpired that the finance department had forgotten to book her hotel. Furious, she contacted the hotel herself, but it was now fully booked. What's more, all the hotels in the vicinity were also fully booked. She had to settle for a distant hotel involving taxi rides to and from the conference venue, instead of being on-site as planned. She was very angry with her finance department who curtly told her that it was her responsibility to check the arrangements. She was furious that she had to check that they hadn't made mistakes, but decided to channel her anger. She decided that the finance department was 'useless', and introduced a tagging system so that she could double-check anything that involved this department. She extended her personal checking system to other situations and departments, and a year on actually felt that some good had come out of the experience.

Channelling anger towards a positive outcome may involve suggestions for change at the organisational level, and this is likely to involve persistence. Other people may be resistant to your ideas for change, particularly in large institutions where things have 'always' been done a particular way. Prepare your case by writing down the proposed scheme and its benefits. Mention your experience, but do not get too emotional about it – the idea is to present rational, not emotion-driven, change. If other people have had similar experience, this evidence can be used to add weight to your argument.

Maintaining the motivation
In trying to channel the anger, you may be lucky and achieve the results you want fairly quickly. If, however, you are taking on a big corporation, you may have to face knock-backs and set-backs. If your initial anger dissipates, it is at this point that you are likely to give up. Remember that anger is the motivating force here and, like most strong emotions, it does tend to fade with time; especially if you have talked about the incident many times with others or relived it in your mind a great deal. Maintaining the motivation to act over a long period of time can become a problem.

There are two ways of looking at this issue. On the one hand, if your motivation has waned, it is likely that your anger has dissipated and in this case you could leave it at that. If you are not angry, why persevere? On the other hand, you might still be determined to effect some change and, in these cases, it can be useful to try and maintain or regenerate the anger. This sounds rather strange advice in an anger management book, but it is advice that serves to remind us that anger is not all bad and destructive – it can be an important motivating source.

Diminished anger can actually be maintained or regenerated by doing some of the same things that you did to get rid of it in the first place! Reliving the experience, rereading your anger diaries, and talking again to people – these are techniques that can induce the emotion to some extent, but only if there has been a time delay since you last engaged in such activities. That is, if a few months have passed since the event and since you talked about it or relived it, engaging in these behaviours can induce the anger again (although not with the same strength as the initial feeling). The resurgence of anger should perpetuate your motivation to act a little longer.

Summary

We have finished looking at anger management techniques today, including ways of channelling your anger towards a positive outcome. Tomorrow we will look at how to manage or deal with other people's anger.

Managing the anger of others at work

So far, we have mainly focused on managing your own anger, but today we look at practical or behavioural ways of coping when other people get angry at work. These 'other people' are likely to be customers, but could just as well be your boss or colleagues. Generally, the sorts of things that other people at work get angry with you for tend to fit within a finite number of themes, depending upon whether that other person is a customer, the boss or a colleague. Issues covered today are:

- Common reasons why customers get angry and practical techniques to deal with them
- Common reasons why the boss gets angry and practical techniques to deal with them
- Common reasons why colleagues get angry and practical techniques to deal with them

Why do customers get angry with you?

Customers' anger generally falls within the following themes:

- *Frustration*: customers get angry when they feel that their attempts to get the result they deserve are continually thwarted. Common causes of frustration are automated telephone answer systems (by the time they actually get through to you they may have been hanging on for a long time, been cut off or got lost in the voice-mail routing system), being passed from department to department (and often having to explain their situation over and over again) and miscommunication (whereby one person tells them one thing but someone else says something contradictory).

- *Believing that you don't care or don't care enough*: customers often feel very emotional about trying to achieve what they consider to be a righting of a wrong. That wrong could be anything from receiving damaged or faulty products and poor service to more serious concerns such as long hospital waiting lists or a product that has caused some harm or expense (such as the washing machine that damages clothes or a food product that makes someone ill). Yet you might have come across the problem dozens of times – just today! It is hard to work up or express the appropriate emotion over and over again, and consequently you can come across as bored and disinterested. There is nothing more likely to raise a customer's hackles than the feeling that they are simply another complaint to be processed, and that nobody cares or even pretends to care.

- *Believing that you are not doing enough to help*: similar to the above, but this time the problem is a perceived unwillingness (or lack of ability) to solve the problem. Standard apologies or referring to 'company policy' (e.g. 'It is against company policy to offer reductions to unhappy hotel guests') are the kind of processes that make customers feel angry at your apparent refusal to do more to help.

- *Complicated complaint procedures*: many companies demand that customers write in with complaints which, in some circumstances, can make customers angry. These include circumstances when the problem needs solving *now* (e.g. a customer who faces missing a flight because check-in has closed 2 minutes ago will not be placated by invitations to write in to complain) or when the financial value of the complaint is small (but the principle high). Companies know that most customers are put off by having to write in and this reduces their apparent volume of complaints; however, it can greatly increase anger and frustration amongst their customer base.

- *Perception of unjust treatment*: the final theme refers to the feeling of being treated unfairly. Customers may feel, rightly or wrongly, that what they are being offered in response to their complaint is unfair. For instance, many would get angry at the offer of some holiday vouchers as recompense for a ruined holiday or at the offer of a free film at a photo developing centre in recompense for lost memories. Often the company feels that the customer is being dealt with fairly, but the customer does not share that view.

Managing customer anger

The angry customer is possibly the hardest situation to diffuse because of the twin demands to both defend the company (or yourself) and obey the 'customer is king' adage. Nevertheless, these demands need not be mutually exclusive. An angry customer who is made to feel valued and respected can not only become calm and cooperative, but can also become a more loyal customer. A customer complaint can be seen as an opportunity to deliver outstanding customer service and retain that customer (and their friends/family) for future repeat business. Here's how:

1 *Work out into which theme the customer's anger fits*: use the above section to identify the source of their anger so that you can deal with it appropriately. Sometimes their irritation might straddle more than one theme. You might need to ask more questions to find out what is really niggling them.

2 *Acknowledge that you understand both the problem* and *the emotion*: this shows that you are listening and appreciate not only the practicalities of the problem, but also how they are feeling about the problem. For example, you could say, 'So, you have been through three people to reach me, you've been cut off once and this has all taken you two days? No wonder you are angry with us!'

3 *Very angry people can be beyond rationality so be wary of asking too many questions at this stage*: making conciliatory or understanding noises is probably the best thing to do: 'I understand', 'That must have been distressing', 'That sounds like a real inconvenience', 'It sounds like you have been sent on a bit of a wild goose chase there.'

4 *Be human; present a human response*: this means expressing

sympathy for the caller, rather than just listening like an automated answering service. This might involve a little acting or pretence, but it can really help defuse the situation.

5 *Let the customer know that you care*: this can be achieved by giving the customer your name, assuring them that they will not need to do anything else – that you will handle everything from now. This is especially helpful to the customer who has made several attempts to get the problem solved already. Call them by their name (always Mr/Mrs/Ms etc.). Reassure them that you will get to the bottom of the problem one way or another, and make sure you follow this through. Offer to call them back at a later stage to check that they are satisfied.

6 *Appear to be on the customer's side*: a customer is less likely to rant at you if they feel that you are with them. Saying things such as 'We're not normally meant to help in this way, but you've had such a rotten time . . .' or, 'My supervisor asked not to be disturbed but I'll risk it' can

really defuse their anger. This can also include acknowledging that the company is not always right and that, for example, its complaints procedures are rather complicated. At the very least, this should deflect their anger away from you.

7 *Agree with them (if appropriate) and apologise*: it is amazing how hard some people find this to do. For many angry customers, a genuine apology is all they want. Even better is an assurance from you that an enquiry into the problem will begin. Moreover, even better than all this is an admission that the customer is right: 'I can't believe the hassle you have had! You are right to be angry and I am so sorry. I will do whatever I personally can, Mr Smith, to put this right.'

By agreeing with the criticism levelled at you, the customer should be completely thrown. This response is usually the last thing they expect and it can really knock all the fury out of them. It is easy to be angry with someone who disagrees with you but when faced with the 'agreement and apologise' response, the customer is simply disarmed and will usually calm down quickly.

N.B. The situation is very different if the customer becomes abusive or aggressive, and these scenarios will be dealt with tomorrow.

Why does your boss get angry with you?

A good manager should be able to express any anger assertively and appropriately, but that is not always the case, and some bosses do scream and shout. There are usually common themes that the boss's anger falls into:

- *You have let them down*: a manager can feel let down for a whole range of reasons. For example, you haven't done what they asked you to do, you haven't done a piece of work to their required standard, you haven't met a deadline, the work is inaccurate, the presentation is poor, etc. The anger can arise from the feeling that their wishes are being ignored, that they are not being attended or listened to properly, or from a perception that you are just incompetent (incompetence in others is often a source of anger).
- *You have caused them extra work*: linked to the above theme is the idea that the boss is going to have to do something to make up for your mistakes. As we all know, an unexpected piece of extra work delays us in getting on with our own projects or even from going home or elsewhere. This is likely to make us stressed, but when there is someone to blame for it, we can turn that emotion into anger and have an outlet for it.
- *You have caused them embarrassment with a client*: imagine if the boss delivers a presentation using data that you have prepared, only for the client to point out that the numbers are wrong. Most people would understand the boss being livid with you. Here, the anger stems from the fact that you have made them look stupid.
- *They feel their position has not been respected*: this source of anger is very common with the manager who is a little insecure about his or her own abilities, power and self-efficacy as a manager. They feel that they have to assert themselves as the 'boss' and are sensitive to any apparent attempts to undermine their authority or usurp their power base. Thus, if you do not behave exactly as required, the anger stems not from frustration at having to

redo work or disappointment at being let down, but from
the fury of what they see as your doubting or weakening
their role as manager. In other words, for these threat-
sensitive individuals, your inaccurate or late report reflects
a lack of respect for them and their authority.

Managing the boss's anger

Many of the techniques that are suggested for dealing with
the angry customer can work for the angry boss too.
However, in this case there is the issue of power and the
power imbalance. Whilst you can always walk away from an
abusive customer or feel reassured that once the encounter is
over you need never interact with that person again, the
same cannot be said for the angry boss. Here is someone who
holds power over you and with whom you wish to nurture
an on-going relationship. Dealing with their wrath has to be
done in such a way as to allow that relationship to continue
undamaged.

Techniques for handling the angry boss include the
following:

1 *Apologise*: this should not be too difficult to do if you were
  in the wrong, but does involve some loss of face. Many
  workers feel that they have to bluff their way through
  mistakes for fear that admission of guilt will damage a
  good impression or reputation. They believe that they
  must deny the mistake or attempt to shift the blame
  elsewhere in order to keep in the boss's good books.
  However, it is more likely that the boss will see through
  these attempts and be disappointed that you are unable to

admit your error. Humans make mistakes and managers are often more impressed by a frank and apologetic admission than pathetic attempts to shift blame.

2 *Defuse the anger with agreement*: nothing disarms the angry person more than complete concurrence. Disagreement fuels anger: when you disagree, the angry person gets more and more frustrated and irritated by their failure to get through to you. By agreeing, the rage dissipates because they have no one to rant against. This technique is especially effective if the boss is particularly furious and beyond reason: 'You are right, I should have been more careful with the figures. I should have double-checked them before I gave them to you. I can't apologise enough.'

3 *Offer explanations but not excuses*: this should not be used when the manager's anger is at its peak; only when he or she is beginning to calm down somewhat. It could perhaps follow an apology. Explanations are very important and, as humans, we have a need to know why: why something has gone wrong, why something has happened, etc.

Offering the explanation is a vital part of the anger defusion process, but if it sounds as if you are making excuses, this can fuel the rage further. You could say, 'What I did was unforgivable and there is no excuse. However, could I just explain how it happened?'

4 *Acknowledge the emotions*: anger is unlikely to be the only emotion that your boss is experiencing. They may be feeling embarrassed because of the poor impression given to a client as a result of your mistake. Alternatively, they could be feeling disappointed or let down or even stressed at the extra work your mistake has caused. It is important, therefore, to acknowledge how they might be feeling to show that you do understand the consequences of what you have done: 'I must have really embarrassed you by getting those figures wrong – I hope you told them it was me, not you, who messed up?'

5 *Reassure the insecure boss*: the manager who feels that your actions reflect a lack of respect for them or their position needs reassuring that this is not the case. This kind of boss may think: 'This person does not listen to me, he doesn't do as I ask him; he just ignores my attempts to manage him. Am I such a poor manager?'

  These kinds of beliefs can lead to the boss lashing out even more in an attempt to exert authority and control, so it is important to offer the reassurance that is craved: 'It must seem like I am not listening to you or taking any notice of you. But, it's not like that at all.'

6 *Suggest ways to repair the damage or to make amends*: the final strategy is to offer a solution or some way of making amends. This could involve you redoing the figures or report, contacting a client to apologise personally, offering to work weekends, etc.

Why do colleagues get angry with you?

The anger of those you work with is likely to fall within the following themes:

- *Your colleagues feel that you are not pulling your weight*: if co-workers feel that, for whatever reason, you are not cooperating as you should or pulling your weight within the team, this can make them angry. It could be that you have genuine reasons such as absence from work due to ill-health, and the perception of you may or may not be justified. Yet the anger stems from the fact that they will have to work extra hard or extra hours to make up for the loss of your input. There may even be resentment that their extra input will not receive any extra credit, or a feeling that you are 'getting away' with slacking.
- *Your colleagues feel that you are getting benefits denied to them*: these benefits could be anything from extra pay and perks to being treated with more leniency by the boss. It could be that you are on a higher pay level, but that your

co-workers do not feel this is justified. Perhaps the boss tolerates late work from you more than from them. Even the perception that the boss likes you more than them can create resentment and anger.

- *You have made a mistake that has caused a colleague problems*: this could range from failure to deliver an important telephone message to giving a colleague inaccurate information for a report. Their anger may stem from a feeling that you have either been too careless and incompetent, or perhaps even deliberately attempted to sabotage them. These perceptions may be unjustified, but remember when the heat rises, rationality is reduced.

- *Office etiquette*: the final theme is bound up with office etiquette, and can include things such as 'borrowing' items from your co-workers' desks (staplers, pens, etc.) and not returning them, leaving the photocopier out of paper or failing to report a fault with it, eating noisy or smelly food in a shared office, engaging in loud personal telephone calls or continually trying to chat when they are attempting to work. All these are sources of irritation, but can quickly lead to full-blown anger.

Managing your colleagues' anger

In many cases you may feel that there is no justification for your colleagues to be angry with you; however, even in these circumstances the onus may still be on you to defuse the situation, if only to make a more pleasant working environment. These tips should help:

1 *Ask them why they are angry*: too often, we don't really know what is eating our colleagues or are unaware of

what we have done to cause offence. Be brave, bite the
bullet and ask.

2 *Eliminate or reduce any anger stimulants*: once you have
figured out what is making your colleagues angry, you
will need to eliminate or reduce these sources of anger.
This might mean speaking to your boss about altering
perceptions of you, changing your workload or changing
the way you behave at work. Of course, this does not mean
that you should passively accept any changes demanded
of you; any changes you make should be in accordance
with your rights (see Tuesday's chapter).

Summary

Today we have looked at the common themes underlying
anger directed towards you from people you encounter at
work. Concentrating specifically on customers, the boss and
colleagues, we have looked at explicit ways of managing this
anger which can be used in conjunction with the general
anger management techniques discussed earlier in this book.
Tomorrow we turn to the more extreme displays of anger
that you might encounter, and examine how to manage more
powerful conflict and aggression.

Managing customer aggression

Angry people do occasionally become aggressive and managing other people's aggression is rather different from managing anger, simply because of the danger to yourself that aggressive people can pose. Today we will examine:

* Signs of impending aggression to watch out for in customers
* Language to prevent aggression escalating
* Techniques to defuse aggression
* Coping with the aftermath

Signs to watch out for

An important aspect of managing aggression is being aware of when a situation might be getting out of hand. Knowing if and when an angry client is likely to turn aggressive is the key to controlling the situation. Once they have become aggressive, they are harder to manage without resorting to physically restraining techniques (such as calling security to have an angry client ejected from your premises or simply putting the phone down on them).

Signs that an angry client might be heading towards aggression include:

* *Previous aggressive episodes*: obviously there are some notorious clients or customers who are known to be aggressive. You should ensure that you have extra support when faced with such a person.
* *Changes in body language*: raised voices, increasing use of

fists (e.g. banging on table) and pointing or jabbing fingers at you are all signs of increasing aggression.

- *Aggressive language*: threats and insults are obvious signs of aggression, but there are other things to watch out for. Threats and insults are often quite personal and made against you as an individual, but the aggressor can also show signs of aggression by depersonalising you and putting you in a group of people against who he or she has a complaint. Examples might be, 'You lot are all the same . . .' or, 'You lot sit there in your cosy offices and haven't a clue about the real world . . .'.

- *Signs of irrationality*: when aggression mounts, thought processes become less rational and this produces many signs that the client is 'losing it'. They may repeat things and keep saying the same things over and over again; they may not seem to take in what you are saying or they may talk faster and stumble and stutter over their words more.

- *A lack of other options*: many people become aggressive when they feel that they have exhausted all other options. Sometimes it is a build-up of sheer frustration that sends them spiralling into aggression, and at other times it is a case of people feeling that if they become aggressive they will get the results they demand. It is thus essential never to leave a client with no further options open to them (see p. 85).

- *Perceived lack of sympathy with their situation*: if the client repeatedly insists that you do not understand their problem, do not understand how they feel, if they maintain that something is simply 'unfair', or they continually complain that you are not giving them the information they want, these are all signs that the client does not feel that you sympathise with them or appreciate

their distress. This can lead to the client wanting to demonstrate just how distressed they are, and this usually means some kind of emotional outburst such as tears or rage.

Use of language to prevent escalating aggression

It is extremely easy to further 'wind up' an angry person with the words and phrases that you use. When that angry person is also aggressive, it is vital that you do not do this. There are key words and phrases that could make your client, customer or patient more aggressive when your goal is to get them to become less aggressive. Here are some of the key things to avoid:

1 *Never tell them to calm down*: of course this is exactly what you want them to do, but saying this is almost guaranteed to further fuel their fury. There are a number of reasons for this. First of all, if the person is not calm, that means that

they have probably lost reason and rationality and are likely to deny that they need to calm down ('I am perfectly calm!', they may shout). Second, it seems to them that you are avoiding the issue that is making them angry in the first place ('Don't tell me to calm down, just do what I want!'). Instead of asking them to calm down, use more precise language, for example, 'Please talk in a softer voice.'

2 *Avoid saying things like, 'You're not going to get anywhere by shouting'*: people often become aggressive when they feel that all their options are exhausted and saying this to them will further frustrate them and make them even more prone to aggression.

3 *Avoid patronising language*: phrases such as, 'With respect . . .' can be seen as patronising. However, there are other ways to be patronising: many people, when faced with angry clients, tend to repeat the same thing over and over again as if they cannot get their message through (e.g., repeating the mantra 'That is against company policy' every time the person requests something); another patronising technique is to say things very slowly as if dealing with a child. All these things can cause aggression to escalate.

4 *Avoid repeating yourself too much*: we talked on Tuesday (p. 40) about using assertive language when dealing with angry people, and one technique is the 'broken record' which involves simply restating the facts or repeating the message over and over. However, be very wary of this when faced with someone who is aggressive. The use of this technique can cause aggression to escalate because it increases their frustration.

5 *Avoid dead-end statements*: these serve to signify to the client

that either there is nothing more they can do or that you are not prepared to help them anymore. You might want to do this to get rid of them and end the conversation, but the client is then left with no options and this can breed aggressive reactions. Common dead-end statements include:

- 'There's nothing more I can do.'
- 'You can't speak to my manager and anyway she would say the same.'
- 'There's no one else you can speak to.'
- 'It is against company policy.'
- 'You can write to Head Office, but they will say the same.'

It is not only what you say and the way that you say it which can aggravate aggression. Your body language can also make a difference. On Tuesday we discussed the importance of maintaining a non-confrontational posture (not direct, face to face), of not invading the aggressor's space, and of avoiding aggressive hand signals.

Techniques to defuse aggression

1 *Be assertive (see Tuesday's chapter)*: this means telling the aggressor that their actions are not acceptable and, if appropriate, why they are not, and giving them an alternative way of behaving. For example, 'Shouting is not acceptable. You are disturbing other people and making me feel uncomfortable. Please speak more quietly.' If you simply asked them to stop shouting without providing an alternative, they would probably immediately shout back,

'I am not shouting!' Don't say 'please' too much because this can make you appear more passive than assertive.

2 *Acknowledge the emotion (see Friday's chapter)*: aggression often escalates when people feel they are not being understood, at least in the terms of the way they feel. It is important to show that you understand or accept their feelings. Examples might be, 'I understand that you are really upset at having missed your flight' or, 'I can see that you are very angry'. Although such statements are likely to see an initial flurry or further rage ('Of course I am angry – what are you going to do about it?!'), continued efforts to demonstrate your understanding should pay off because this can send the message that their anger (but not their aggression) is understandable and even acceptable.

3 *Change the environment*: this is not always possible, but if it is, try and take the aggressor to a new environment. This is especially important if the person is being aggressive in front of others before whom they would lose face by calming down. Also, changing the environment can be a

distraction and give time and space for the aggressor to calm down. Naturally, you should not place yourself at risk or use physical contact.

The way you request the move (to another office perhaps) has to be handled with care because the aggressor may think that you want to avoid a 'scene', which they might be keen on making. Suggesting that the complaint is serious enough to warrant special attention is the best way to deal with this. For example, 'I can see how angry you are and I want to help you. Let's go into my office where I will be able to get access to the extra information I need.'

4 *Give them options*: as mentioned before, people are more likely to get aggressive when they feel that they have reached the end of the road and there are no alternatives left. Meeting a brick wall of resistance is very frustrating for anyone, even more so for those who have difficulty controlling their anger. Instead of using dead-end statements with aggressive people, do all you can to assure them that they have not reached the end of the road (even if they have). Care should be taken here; someone who has been given a dead-end statement and then turns aggressive should not be suddenly told that there is something that can be done for them after all. It is obviously not a good idea to backtrack and appear to reward the aggression (particularly in view of other customers). Instead, it might simply be a case of giving them the options that are available, even if they are not desirable ones. For example, you could give them the name and address of the customer service manager at head office or a complaints form (always better than just vaguely telling them to write to head office) or you could

offer to go and 'check' with your superiors, or you could
repeat any earlier offers to solve the problem.

5 *Make notes*: it is amazing how powerful the simple act of
writing in a notebook can be. It sends the message that the
person is being taken seriously, is being listened to, and
that their comments and complaints will be passed on.
This is also a useful way of telling an aggressor that any
abuse will be recorded. (Do be careful that they do not
think that the notes are only for recording abuse because
this can increase anger, not decrease it.)

6 *Distraction techniques*: it might sometimes be possible to
draw the aggressor into a conversation about something
related but less confrontational (see box below for
example).

Kate was a hospital receptionist in Accident and
Emergency and was approached by a patient who was
furious to be kept waiting so long. He began to get
aggressive, demanding to know when he would be
seen by a doctor. Kate asked him if he had ever been
to this A&E Department on a previous occasion and,
somewhat taken aback by the change in direction of
her conversation, he said that he hadn't but that he had
been to another department. 'What was the wait like
there?', she asked. 'Just as bad,' he replied angrily, 'I
had to wait two hours to have my chest seen to.' He
then went on to tell her that his grandson had
accompanied him that time – a piece of information that
gave Kate the chance to lead him on to less
confrontational topics. She asked after his grandson. 'Is
he at work now? And she let the patient talk about the

boy for a while. This calmed the patient down and
distracted him from his complaint long enough to listen
to Kate's explanation of why it was all taking so long.

7 *Leave the situation*: this could mean bringing the
conversation to a temporary or permanent close.
Aggressive callers on the phone can be told that you are
going to check something out and will get back to them.
Whether you do or not depends on just how aggressive or
abusive they have been. Face-to-face contacts can be ended
by making excuses such as, 'I will just go and get my
notebook/laptop, etc.' A temporary break in the
conversation can give the client time to reflect on their
position and calm down on their own. It can also give you
time to take stock and decide what to do next.

Dealing with the aftermath of aggression

An aggressive episode at work can have a significant
psychological impact on you by leaving you feeling stressed
and/or angry. Common emotions experienced after an
aggressive episode include:

- Anger towards the perpetrator about the abuse you
  have experienced
- Resentment towards your organisation which has
  put you in this position, and which you may feel has
  not given you adequate protection

- Resentment towards colleagues or managers who were not there when needed
- Regret that you did not handle things differently
- Fear about the way things may have turned out

It is common to:

- Repeatedly go over the episode in your mind, reliving what happened and what might have happened
- Feel increased vulnerability not just in your place of work, but in other situations too
- Feel a heightened sense of awareness about the perceived risk of situations

All of these are normal reactions in the immediate aftermath of an aggressive episode and can last days or weeks depending on the severity of the incident and the make-up of the 'victim'. The psychological impact can be managed by taking the following steps:

- Accept that you might experience the emotions outlined above. Acknowledge that these are normal reactions and that they will dissipate with time.
- Have some sort of outlet for your feelings. This could be writing down what happened and how you felt or talking to colleagues and friends. This is healthier than bottling it up.
- Your organisation should have some sort of incident procedure for reporting and dealing with experiences

like this. Good procedures include debriefing (perhaps by counsellors) and measures to consider the antecedents, behaviour and consequences of the event in order to reduce the risk of it either happening again or having the same impact. If your organisation does not have such procedures (perhaps because the incident was so unexpected), you could possibly use your experiences to do something positive by helping to develop better procedures (including risk assessment).

A good text for further reading, particularly for those in health or social care settings, is *Managing Aggression* by Ray Braithwaite (1999, Routledge).

Summary

We have ended the week by looking at the most challenging form of anger management – coping when customers become aggressive towards you at work. We have looked at various techniques to defuse the anger and prevent the aggression escalating, as well as how to cope with the aftermath of such distressing episodes. Extreme incidents are relatively rare of course, but hopefully by now you have a whole range of skills in your tool-box to draw on to cope with almost any anger-eliciting situation. Good luck!

FURTHER READING

Polly Bird, *Teach Yourself Time Management*, 2003, London: Hodder & Stoughton.

Ray Braithwaite, *Managing Aggression*, 1999, London: Routledge.

Richard Craze, *Teach Yourself Relaxation*, 2003, London: Hodder & Stoughton.

Naomi Ozaniec, *Teach Yourself Meditation*, 2003, London: Hodder & Stoughton.

Declan Treacy and Polly Bird, *Time Management In a Week*, 2002, London: Hodder & Stoughton.

For information

on other

IN A WEEK titles

go to

www.inaweek.co.uk